DRUG DEPENDENCE

DRUG DEPENDENCE

L. H. Colligan

 Marshall Cavendish
Benchmark
New York

Special thanks to John Roll, professor and associate dean for research, director of the program of excellence in the addictions at Washington State University College of Nursing, for his expert review of the manuscript

Published by Marshall Cavendish Benchmark
An imprint of Marshall Cavendish Corporation

This publication represents the opinions and views of the author based on L. H. Colligan's personal experience, knowledge, and research. The information in this book serves as a general guide only. The author and publisher have used their best efforts in preparing this book and disclaim liability rising directly and indirectly from the use and application of this book.

Other Marshall Cavendish Offices:
Marshall Cavendish International (Asia) Private Limited, 1 New Industrial Road, Singapore 536196 • Marshall Cavendish International (Thailand) Co Ltd. 253 Asoke, 12th Flr, Sukhumvit 21 Road, Klongtoey Nua, Wattana, Bangkok 10110, Thailand • Marshall Cavendish (Malaysia) Sdn Bhd, Times Subang, Lot 46, Subang Hi-Tech Industrial Park, Batu Tiga, 40000 Shah Alam, Selangor Darul Ehsan, Malaysia

Marshall Cavendish is a trademark of Times Publishing Limited

This book is not intended for use as a substitute for advice, consultation, or treatment by a licensed medical practitioner. The reader is advised that no action of a medical nature should be taken without consultation with a licensed medical practitioner, including action that may seem to be indicated by the contents of this work, since individual circumstances vary and medical standards, knowledge, and practices change with time. The publisher, author, and medical consultants disclaim all liability and cannot be held responsible for any problems that may arise from the use of this book.

All websites were available and accurate when this book was sent to press.

Library of Congress Cataloging-in-Publication Data

Colligan, L. H.
  Drug dependence / by L.H. Colligan.
      p. cm. — (Health alert)
  Summary: "Provides comprehensive information on the causes, treatment, and history of drug dependence"—Provided by publisher.
  Includes index.
  ISBN 978-0-7614-4818-1
  1. Drug addiction—Juvenile literature. I. Title.
  RC564.3.C65 2011
  616.86—dc22
                                          2009051255

Editor: Joy Bean
Publisher: Michelle Bisson
Art Director: Anahid Hamparian

Photo research by Candlepants Incorporated
Cover Photo: allOver photography / Alamy Images
The photographs in this book are used by permission and through the courtesy of:
Getty Images: David Young-Wolff, 3, 7; John Glover, 5, 32; Brad Wilson, 11; 3D4Medical.com, 14; Nucleus Medical Art, Inc., 15; Dorling Kindersley, 18; Penny Tweedie, 20; Daryl Solomon, 22; Ron Levine, 24; Peter Dazeley, 27; Steven Puetzer, 42; Don Smetzer, 46; Josef Fankhauser, 51. *Alamy Images*: David Hoffman Photo Library, 30; Peter Titmuss, 37; Angela Hampton Picture Library, 49; Jeff Greenberg, 52. *Art Resource, NY*: Image Select, 36. *The Bridgeman Art Library*: Private Collection / Peter Newark American Pictures, 38.

Printed in Malaysia (T)
6 5 4 3 2 1

CONTENTS

Chapter 1	What Is It Like to Be Drug Dependent?	6
Chapter 2	What Is Drug Dependence?	12
Chapter 3	The History of Drug Dependence	34
Chapter 4	From Drug Dependence to Independence	44
	Glossary	55
	Find Out More	59
	Index	61

WHAT IS IT LIKE TO BE DRUG DEPENDENT?

Fifteen-year-old Melissa found out she had a **drug** problem when she tried to quit smoking. To her surprise, Melissa had become **dependent** on **nicotine**, the main drug in cigarettes. And she wanted to get unhooked from it. In health class she had learned that drugs are chemicals that change what happens inside your brain. Nicotine sure felt that way.

Melissa hardly looked like someone who was hooked on a drug. She had had her first cigarette at a summer ballet camp with older dancers. "After a day of really hard classes, it was just fun to go walking in the woods and hang out with the new girls I met. I was pretty surprised when I saw some of them light up. Nobody forced me to take my first cigarette. It just happened. I still cannot believe how fast I got hooked," Melissa says.

Trying cigarettes for the first time was Melissa's biggest mistake. Once she started smoking, she felt like she could not stop.

Melissa knew her parents would be incredibly disappointed and upset that she smoked. She figured she would quit smoking as soon as ballet camp ended. But things did not work out that way. When Melissa started high school that fall, she discovered that a couple of her other friends had started smoking over the summer, too.

Melissa was careful about her smoking, so her parents never caught on—but her younger sister did. "That is when I knew I had to quit," Melissa says. "Carrie looked up to me. She wanted to be like me. I told Carrie I was going to quit and asked her not to tell."

Melissa tried to stop smoking twice but failed. Going without cigarettes made her jittery. Then her friend Kate decided to quit, too. Together, they took baby steps. First, they stopped buying cigarettes. Then they began to hang out in places where they would not be tempted to smoke. Melissa got herself down to a couple of borrowed cigarettes a week. The day before her birthday, Melissa announced to Kate and her sister that she was going to have her last cigarette.

"I have been fifteen years old for fifty-two days," Melissa says. "That is the same amount of time I have not smoked. I wish I could say I never wanted another cigarette, but sometimes I still do. When that happens, I get busy with something else—knitting, yoga, or walking the half mile to Kate's house. She is on day forty of not smoking. And my sister, Carrie, is on day zero. She said she is never going to smoke after seeing what I went through."

Fourteen-year-old Will did not want to be pudgy when he started high school. At his school physical, he listened closely to what the nurse said about eating right and getting more exercise. He decided to join a gym and start working out.

Exercise and giving up junk food soon helped Will slim down over the summer. So did getting taller. People started saying, "Hey, Will, you look good." The more compliments Will got, the more he worked out. But he still thought of himself as a flabby, overweight kid. He wished he had one of those bodybuilding shapes he saw on some older guys who worked out, too.

Will made a new friend at the gym. Andy was on the junior varsity football team at the high school. He suggested that Will try out, so he did. Will was amazed when he made the team. Will wondered whether he could ever look like some of his muscular teammates.

Will soon found a way when Andy handed him some pills. "They are sort of muscle vitamins," Andy said. "They really work. A bunch of the varsity guys take them. That is where I got them. Only Coach is not in on it."

"Are they **steroids**?" Will asked Andy. "I heard they can cause all kinds of problems."

"Hey, look at me," Andy said. "Our bodies make steroids

anyway. The pills just give a boost to what you already have."

Will decided to try the pills. He told himself he would just use them for the rest of the season. He would quit once he built up his muscles enough. Nothing seemed to happen for a while, but eventually Will did get bigger muscles. Was it a coincidence that he also seemed to be playing better football? By the time the season ended, Will was placing orders for the pills with Andy.

Off-season, Will kept taking steroids. Then a couple of things happened. His face broke out in pimples. When he went to get his skin checked, Will's doctor asked Will if he was taking steroids. Will said no but wondered if the doctor could tell he was lying. Will did not want anybody at home to find out. He was fighting a lot with his parents and blowing up over nothing all the time. Will knew steroids could affect his mood, but he did not care.

Then the worst thing happened. Will's mother found his steroid pills in his gym bag. They had the biggest blowup ever! Will's parents immediately took him to the family doctor to talk about his drug dependence. Will found out that artificial steroids had caused some of the hair loss he had been having, as well as his bad skin. Will learned that steroids also affect growth and sexual **hormones**. The doctor made an appointment for Will to visit a counselor. Will needed help because he still felt he was overweight and out of shape. The counselor helped Will to see that he had a body image problem.

In order to get bigger muscles fast, Will started to take steroids.

Will's family doctor supervised Will's gradual steroid **withdrawal** so his body could get back to normal. Luckily, Will had not been taking large amounts of the drug. He had some headaches and stomachaches. He felt pretty tired for a few weeks. It was off-season, though, so Will got through the withdrawal period okay. It took him awhile longer to stop seeing himself as a pudgy kid. But by the time football season came around again, Will was in good shape for anything.

2

WHAT IS DRUG DEPENDENCE?

Drug dependence is a desire to keep using a chemical substance despite the harm it may cause. For example, a drug-dependent student might keep taking **amphetamine** pills, commonly called speed, to try to improve her focus at school. A college student may frequently smoke **marijuana** despite the risk of being arrested and kicked out of school. A teen might keep drinking **alcohol** even though his drunken behavior is driving away good friends.

These drug users mainly experience **psychological** symptoms, such as **anxiety** and a desire to keep taking their drug. They have not yet become drug **addicts**, who suffer intense psychological and physical withdrawal symptoms without their drug. But drug dependence and drug addiction are related. Drug addicts start out being drug dependent first. For both kinds of drug users, it all starts in the head.

THE HEALTHY BRAIN

What does a healthy, drug-free brain do? This 3-pound organ is the body's control center. If your body were a computer, the brain would be its hard drive. You would not want to spill anything on the hard drive because it would affect all the workings of the computer. Because drugs change the brain, they affect the workings of the rest of the body.

To work well, the brain needs healthy amounts of food, water, sleep, and oxygen. Day and night, the brain releases natural chemicals that make cells—the tiniest living parts of the body—do their jobs. A healthy brain controls breathing, growth, blood pressure, movement, body temperature, thoughts, moods, and much more.

The brain performs these tasks when its nerve cells, called **neurons**, send chemical messengers called **neurotransmitters** to all parts of the body. Neurotransmitters pass along messages from the brain. They may tell muscle cells to start shivering or heart cells to pump harder.

One major neurotransmitter is **dopamine**. This brain chemical triggers desires and pleasurable feelings so that an organism will drink water, eat, and reproduce. Another neurotransmitter, called **serotonin**, sends signals that the body has had enough water, food, or sex. Serotonin also regulates moods. Both dopamine and serotonin are involved with the brain's reward center, or **pleasure circuit**.

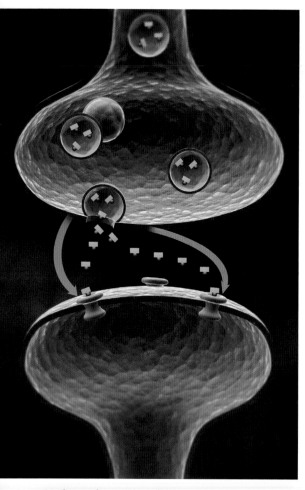

As dopamine moves from neuron to neuron, it affects awareness, pleasure, pain, movement, sleep, moods, attention levels, and memory.

All animals, including humans, have a pleasure circuit. Dopamine in the reward center causes humans and other animals to build up memories of positive physical sensations, such as the pleasure of drinking water after being thirsty or eating food after being hungry. The brain connections among pleasure, memory, and the senses cause cravings for anything that made dopamine flow in the past. That includes drugs. Brain scans have shown that when a smoker sees a photo of someone with a cigarette, brain areas involved in automatic learning (such as learning to ride a bike or to brush teeth) become active.

For preteens and teenagers, one area of the pleasure circuit—the **nucleus accumbens**—behaves differently from that of young children and adults. Using brain-imaging machines, researchers have observed something amazing in teen brains. These brains show a stronger response to rewards than the brains of adults and young children do. This is probably the brain's way of making sure young people repeat actions they need to survive to adulthood.

In one way, however, this heightened reward response happens at a bad age. Teens are often exposed to drugs at the same time that their brains are still under construction. The brain's **frontal lobe** is involved in judgment, decision making, and planning for the future. This area does not mature completely until young people reach their mid-twenties. Since drug use changes the brain, negative changes may get "wired" in to the frontal lobe. That makes drug taking much riskier for teens than for any other age group. Nine out of ten adult smokers started smoking before they were eighteen. The great majority of alcoholics began their drinking habits before they were fifteen. These are the reasons why there are laws against selling cigarettes to

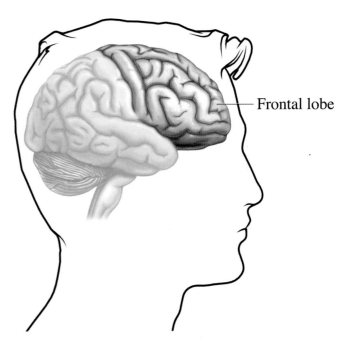

Frontal lobe

Drug use at an early age harms the brain's frontal lobe, which does not mature until someone's early twenties.

people under eighteen and selling alcohol to people under twenty-one.

THE BRAIN AND BODY ON DRUGS

Many drugs enter the brain despite a thin protective covering called the **blood-brain barrier**. This fatty layer usually does a good job of screening out foreign substances that might harm the brain. So how do drugs get past that barrier? They fake it! Some drug ingredients, such as those in marijuana and manufactured drug chemicals, look like natural chemicals that the brain produces. As copycats, many drug chemicals latch on to brain cell **receptors** the way a copy of a key fits in a lock. The drugs trick brain neurons into releasing more dopamine and other brain chemicals than they usually do.

An increase in dopamine causes pleasant feelings way beyond normal levels. But higher dopamine levels also cause big problems. The body needs normal levels of dopamine to carry out its activities. The brain responds to excess dopamine by slowing down production of the chemical, so the drug user crashes. In addition, the drug user will begin to need more of the drug just to experience that first dopamine-generated "high" (the intense pleasurable state the user had when he or she first tried the drug). The need for more of a drug than a person needed before is called **tolerance**. It is a sign of drug addiction.

Someone who goes on to become drug dependent or drug addicted usually begins with drugs that are fairly easy to get—cigarettes, alcohol, marijuana, **inhalants**, or **prescription** pills that belong to someone else. Users who become drug dependent usually try these drugs for the first time in their early teens. They may be searching for a drug that will make them feel excited or one that will calm them down.

STIMULANTS

Drugs that speed up the brain and body are called **stimulants**. They can be inhaled, snorted through the nose, swallowed in pill form, or injected with a needle. Inhaled stimulants, such as the nicotine in cigarettes, **cocaine**, and **methamphetamine**, enter the body faster than other types of stimulants.

Someone taking a stimulant feels more energetic, alert, talkative, focused, and awake than usual. Who would not want to feel that way? Unfortunately, that would be like driving a car at 120 miles an hour all the time. The human body is not designed to be in overdrive. Normally, the body maintains a state called **homeostasis**. This means the brain's natural chemicals balance sleep-wake cycles, growth, alertness, moods, digestion, breathing, blood circulation, and much more.

All drugs affect the body's homeostasis. Stimulants cause a surge in dopamine. The drug-taking experience may feel pleasurable to the user, but the body pays a big price. Repeated

Ninety percent of cocaine abusers began their drug use with cigarettes, alcohol, or marijuana. Cocaine is a highly addictive stimulant.

stimulant use harms all cells. Damaged, worn-out cells put the body at risk of premature aging, irregular heartbeat, infection, cancer, and many other illnesses. Like all drugs, stimulants change moods. The "up" mood is usually followed by an anxious and tired mood.

The danger of all stimulants is that their quick, pleasurable effects create cravings that may lead to drug dependence.

NICOTINE

After **caffeine**, nicotine is the most widely used stimulant *and* **depressant**. Nicotine, a chemical in tobacco leaves, acts on the same "feel-good" part of the brain as other stimulants, such as cocaine and amphetamines. But like depressants, such as alcohol, nicotine also slows down activity in the **central nervous system (CNS)**. This slowdown produces a feeling of relaxation after just a few cigarettes.

The effects of smoking one cigarette begin within ten to fifteen seconds of inhalation and wear off in less than an hour. Cigarettes deliver a double hit to the brain. Nicotine not only hooks new smokers quickly, it also slows the release of brain chemicals that say, "Enough!" That is not good news, since smokers put themselves at risk for the following conditions:

- premature aging
- reduced height in boys (girls mature physically more quickly than boys and usually have finished growing before they start smoking)
- obesity, especially in older smokers
- reproductive cancers in the testicles, ovaries, and breasts
- lung cancer
- ongoing heart and lung disease

- earlier death than nonsmokers (by thirteen to fourteen years)

As a stimulant and a depressant, nicotine, along with other tobacco toxins, increases the heart rate but slows down blood clotting. Tobacco chemicals temporarily improve concentration but slow down breathing. Over time, nicotine and other tobacco toxins kill lung cells and tiny, hairlike structures that sweep up dust and other foreign particles that get inside the lungs.

Experts consider cigarettes to be the most common **gateway drug** leading to the use of outlawed, **illicit** drugs. According

Cigarette companies raised the nicotine levels in cigarettes about 1.6 percent a year between 1998 and 2005. Nicotine is as addictive as heroin and cocaine.

Smokers and Aging

. . . .

What would you do if you heard of a product that promised to give you more wrinkles, more gray hair, and early hair loss? Would you buy it? Well, about 19 percent of Americans do buy that product: cigarettes. A 2008 study published in the *British Journal of Medicine* found a significant link between smoking and early graying and baldness. Many studies also have shown that smokers have paler, more wrinkled skin than nonsmokers do.

There is a scientific reason for this. Toxic chemicals in smoke narrow blood vessels. This slows down the flow of oxygen and nutrients that skin needs to stay firm and healthy. Smoking is associated with a breakdown of skin fibers, which causes the skin to droop. Toxins in smoke also seem to damage hair follicles—small, nourishing glands on the scalp from which hair grows. This causes hair loss as well as the loss of the original hair color.

to the National Institute on Drug Abuse (NIDA), the great majority of teens who go on to use alcohol, marijuana, and cocaine start out by smoking cigarettes. Smoking becomes a gateway activity because underage smokers do something that is illegal for their age group. Smoking teaches these users that an illicit substance is a quick fix for boredom or difficult feelings.

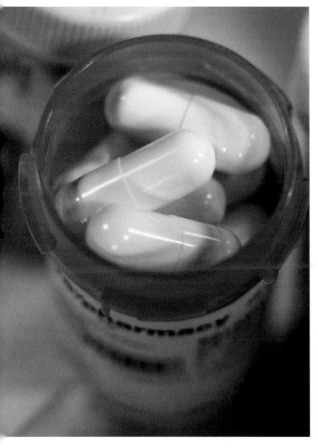

Some people abuse prescription medication and become addicted to them.

AMPHETAMINES

Doctors regularly—and legally—prescribe amphetamines, such as Adderall and Ritalin, to students with **attention-deficit/hyperactivity disorder (ADHD)**. As prescribed, these amphetamines release just enough dopamine in a part of the brain that boosts concentration. These effects may take about a week to begin.

Illicit amphetamine use is a big drug problem, however. Some teenagers and young adults take amphetamines without a prescription, in unsupervised doses and methods, to become more focused and awake than they normally would be. These illicit users may feel that schoolwork is too difficult to manage without the extra boost that amphetamines give them. However, uncontrolled and unprescribed stimulants have many side effects, including increased heart rate and blood pressure, sleeplessness, moodiness, anxiety, and dependence.

COCAINE

This highly addictive stimulant is made from the leaves of the coca plant. Because it is usually snorted as a powder through the nose, cocaine reaches the brain within seconds. The brain floods the system with feel-good neurotransmitters and temporarily prevents them from returning to the original neurons. Cocaine causes pleasurable feelings of **euphoria**. The effects last about an hour.

The wild swings between cocaine highs and lows lead to cravings for more cocaine as the user tries to avoid the crash. This may quickly set off a fast cycle of drug dependence, which can lead to full-blown cocaine addiction. Many cocaine addicts sacrifice relationships, money, school, jobs, and health to continue using their drug. Recent research has shown that the brain of a cocaine addict is abnormally thin in the cortex. This is the area that controls judgment, attention, and decision making. Other researchers have found that cocaine use damages cells in the pleasure circuit, which increases the risk of **depression**. Cocaine overdoses cause serious heart and breathing problems which can lead to emergency room visits and sometimes death. Cocaine combined with alcohol can be deadly.

CAFFEINE

Most types of coffee and tea, certain soft drinks, energy drinks, and many over-the-counter painkillers contain caffeine, a mild stimulant. A caffeinated drink makes someone feel alert within

Drinking a cup of coffee every morning may seem harmless, but the caffeine in coffee can cause dependency.

a half hour of drinking it. The effect can last for around three hours. Many people become dependent on the caffeine in coffee and energy drinks.

Caffeine disrupts healthy sleep cycles that control children's and teens' growth hormones. People who get hooked on caffeinated drinks often miss out on nutritious, bone-building drinks such as milk and juice. Caffeinated soft drinks and energy drinks are loaded with sugar or sugar substitutes. These often replace healthier foods and beverages that growing bodies need. Coffee, soft drinks, and energy drinks stain teeth and cause tooth decay. This is a high cost for a quick buzz. Children and teens can get the energy they need by eating right, drinking plenty of water, exercising, and getting enough sleep.

DEPRESSANTS

Depressants are drugs that cause a slowdown in normal activities of the brain and the rest of the body. Depressants change sleep-wake cycles and affect areas of the brain involved in judgment and behavior. Chemicals in depressants cause sleepiness, confusion, poor memory, weak muscles, and garbled speech. Someone under the influence of depressants should not bike, skateboard, Rollerblade, swim, play any other risky sports, or operate a vehicle.

Depressants act on the receptors of a neurotransmitter called **gamma-aminobutyric acid (GABA)**. GABA helps relax muscles and promote sleep. People take depressants to feel relaxed and calm. A desire to experience this relaxed state repeatedly is a sign of dependence on depressants. Although depressants seem to relieve symptoms of depression, overuse of them actually masks depression and makes it worse.

ALCOHOL

Alcohol is the most widely used depressant. One alcoholic drink—a glass of wine, a can of beer, an ounce or so of hard liquor—affects the brain in ninety seconds. The effects of that drink last an hour or so.

Because alcohol makes many people feel lively and outgoing, most drinkers have no idea that alcohol is a depressant. Alcohol slows down activities in many parts of the brain. One is the area that makes people shy and careful. When alcohol depresses cautious feelings, people may say or do foolish, careless, or risky things that they would never say or do if they were not drinking.

Alcohol slows reaction time and concentration as well. People who have an alcohol blood level higher than 0.08 percent cannot drive safely, type accurately, play a sport with coordination, or perform many other tasks they can do well when sober. The chemicals in alcohol depress speech and motor centers, so drinkers start to stumble and mumble. Alcohol also slows down the digestive system. Very drunk people vomit

Alcohol affects many parts of the body. It can make people do things they might not normally do.

when their digestive systems slow down so much that they cannot digest food. When they overdose, drinkers become unconscious as their breathing and heart rate slow down dangerously. Some drinkers die because they overdose on alcohol or combine it with other drugs.

Binge drinking—drinking more than four to five drinks in an hour—drastically affects the brain. Here are just some of the effects of repeated binge drinking or frequent nonbinge drinking:

- destruction of cells in the undeveloped brains of teen-agers, particularly in the hippocampus area where memories form
- decrease in brain size
- decrease in brain memory cells
- slowdown in bone and muscle growth in teens, particularly boys, if they begin alcohol use before they finish growing
- obesity
- increased depression and mood changes
- poor judgment and decision making
- accidents
- poor schoolwork
- poor performance on the job

Alcohol dependence develops as it does with most drugs. Users need increased amounts of alcohol to achieve the temporary effects they first experienced.

PAINKILLERS, TRANQUILIZERS, AND SEDATIVES

When prescribed by a doctor, certain medications called **narcotics** can help people endure the pain of surgery, cancer, arthritis, back pain, injuries, severe coughing, sleeplessness, and severe anxiety. Manufactured **opioids** include Vicodin, OxyContin, and certain prescription cough medicines. Their effects—pain relief and a deep sense of calm—are similar to those of **opium**-based **morphine** and **heroin**.

The body produces small amounts of natural opioid chemicals. They attach to opioid receptors on certain cells in the central nervous system. Drug opioids—morphine, heroin, and prescription painkillers—mimic natural opioids. However, these opioid drugs release unnaturally high quantities of dopamine. This excess dopamine causes the body to slow down natural dopamine production. The user then craves more and more of the drug. Doctors carefully monitor opioid use in patients who need pain treatment so that they do not develop uncontrollable cravings and tolerance.

Abuse of calming prescription **tranquilizers**, such as sleeping pills and certain cough syrups, is increasing among young drug users. Antianxiety medications, such as Xanax, relieve anxiety and **panic attacks**. Xanax and other tranquilizers are extremely habit-forming, however. The user soon needs more of the drug more often than when it was originally prescribed.

Opioids and tranquilizers behave as many depressants do. They slow down breathing, motor and speech centers, judgment, and reaction time. Overuse of these drugs can cause digestive problems, hearing loss, and mood swings. The danger of overdosing is high among users who mix opioids with other drugs, such as **sedatives** or alcohol. Users who develop tolerance, or stop the drug, and then restart it are at high risk for opioid overdose.

INHALANTS

Toxic inhalants can be found under bathroom and kitchen sinks, in garages, in basements, and at art supply stores. This makes them accessible to risk-taking preteens who huff, or breathe in, the dangerous chemical fumes. Paint, paint remover, glue, butane cigarette lighters, gasoline, and many aerosol products produce inhalant fumes.

Inhaled fumes act on the brain within seconds. Inhalant users may experience brief **hallucinations**, which are feelings of unreality and excitement. These effects last just a few

Inhaled fumes of over-the-counter products such a glue and spray paint can quickly affect every cell in the body.

minutes, so users often keep inhaling to make the effects last longer.

The longer the toxic gases are in the user's system, the more damage they do. Chemicals in these deadly fumes replace the body's oxygen. Breathing, heartbeat, organ function, and muscle function all slow down. The user slurs words and becomes dizzy or drowsy. Some inhalant users lose consciousness, suffocate, or suffer sudden death due to lack of oxygen or overwhelming tissue damage in vital organs. Chemicals that can dissolve paint, clean deep stains, kill bugs, or fuel a cigarette lighter can destroy brain, lung, muscle, and even eye tissue for good. Inhalants can cause permanent brain damage, breathing problems, nerve and muscle disorders, and brain disruptions called **seizures**.

MARIJUANA

From the teen years onward, the most widely used illegal drug is marijuana, also called pot or weed. Marijuana is more likely than nicotine or alcohol to cause psychological (rather than physical) dependence or addiction.

Marijuana is a **hallucinogen** made from the cannabis plant. When inhaled, marijuana reaches the brain within seconds. Its active ingredient, a chemical called THC, sets off a flood of dopamine in the pleasure circuit. As soon as marijuana smoke reaches the brain, the user's heart beats faster. Blood vessels in the eyes expand, as do bronchial passages that lead

THC, the active ingredient in marijuana, comes from the plant's flowers and dried leaves. THC, and parts of it, can stay in the body for up to several days or weeks.

to the lungs. At first, the user may feel extremely relaxed and experience sights and sounds intensely. Time seems to slow down. Muscle coordination and reaction times also slow down. Between 6 and 11 percent of drivers involved in car accidents test positive for marijuana use.

A 2008 meeting of the American Academy of Pediatrics in Boston, Massachusetts, reported the following:

". . . chronic, heavy marijuana use during adolescence—a critical period of ongoing brain development—is associated with poorer performance on thinking tasks, including slower psychomotor speed and poorer complex attention, verbal memory and planning ability . . . that's evident even after a month of stopping marijuana use."

Marijuana is loaded with harmful toxins. It contains more than twenty times the amount of ammonia, a dangerous chemical, that cigarettes do. In addition, marijuana chemicals remain in the body for up to ten days after the first use. That means it has time to cause more harm than some other drugs.

STEROIDS

Most male teens would start to worry if their faces suddenly developed a lot of pimples, started to lose their hair, or developed breast tissue. Girls would probably be alarmed if they suddenly developed deeper voices or grew dark facial hair. Still, some young people deliberately take artificial steroids that can cause these alarming symptoms. Anabolic steroid users want to build up their muscles and strength. Muscle growth—as well as negative side effects—usually begins about six to twelve weeks after someone starts using steroids.

Anabolic steroids are manufactured versions of sex hormones that a healthy body makes naturally. Steroids change muscle and bone cells in a way that promotes growth. They attach to the body's own steroid receptors and change the signals that the cells send to muscles and bones. Natural steroids help a body grow to full size and develop normal sexual characteristics. Anabolic steroids upset that healthy hormone balance and begin to cause a mix-up in sexual characteristics. Steroid use can affect the workings of the reproductive system.

The majority of steroid users are males, but some females take them, too. Both genders are at risk of developing liver tumors, high blood pressure, heart problems, mood disorders such as aggression and depression, and changes in sexual characteristics.

3

THE HISTORY OF DRUG DEPENDENCE

Drug dependence likely began around six thousand years ago in what is now the Middle East. That is when humans in many parts of the world began to grow **psychoactive** plants for food and medications instead of gathering the plants in the wild. Such early crops included grapes, grains, and wheat grasses. People would **ferment** these plants to make wine and beer.

Later, societies around the world learned to cultivate plants to make opium, marijuana, cocaine, and tobacco products. Thanks to farming, early agricultural societies had more psychoactive plants on hand. Increased availability raised the odds of drug dependence.

ALCOHOL DEPENDENCE

The earliest farmers discovered many benefits in cultivating wild grapes, rice, grains, wheat, and honey. These crops fed growing populations. Alcohol, which kills many germs, provided an alternative to unsanitary drinking water. Loaded with sugar, alcohol supplied calories to fuel the energy needs of people who did backbreaking farmwork. Alcohol also served as a fairly effective painkiller. Finally, drinking wine or beer and eating together were relaxing, bonding social experiences just as they are today.

Early warnings and laws suggest that ancient societies in Egypt, China, Greece, and Rome tried to control alcohol use to prevent dependence. The ancient Babylonian king, Hammurabi (1795–1750 B.C.E.) created regulations for public drinking houses. To this day, countries around the world still restrict when and where alcohol can be sold in taverns and bars. Warnings against the excessive use of alcohol appear in the Old and New Testaments of the Bible. The Muslim Koran completely forbids the drinking of alcohol.

From the early 1500s to the late 1600s, religious and royal leaders in England and Europe viewed excessive drinking as a threat to society. One aide to Henri IV in France told the king that drinking ". . . all too often ruins homes and families."

In the 1800s in England and the United States, waves of people left farms to work in city factories. Public drunkenness

"Just Say No" to Drugs Timeline

. . . .

2000 B.C.E.: An Egyptian priest tells a student, "I, thy superior, forbid thee to go to the taverns." This is one of the earliest known cases of a ruler forbidding someone to take a drug.

625 C.E.: Prophet Muhammad forbids followers of Islam to drink alcohol.

1600s: The Russian czar threatens to torture anyone caught with tobacco.

1736: In England, the Gin Act raises the price of alcohol to keep people from drinking too much. The act does little to decrease alcohol abuse.

1792: China tries to outlaw nonmedicinal use of opium without much success.

An illustration of an opium den in Paris in 1903.

1868: In England, the Poisons and Pharmacy Act forbids anyone without a license to sell opium and other drugs.

1909: Opium smoking becomes a crime in the United States.

1914: The Harrison Narcotic Act controls the sale of opiates and cocaine in the United States.

1920–1933: The sale of alcohol is forbidden during the Prohibition years in the United States. Canada also prohibits alcohol during the periods from 1900 to 1948.

1961: The United Nations urges member states to control cocaine and opiates according to the Single Convention on Narcotic Drugs.

1969: The United States waged the War on Drugs, in which the military attempted to stop illegal drug trade of cocaine, heroin, and marijuana.

1971: The United Nations urges member states to control man-made amphetamines and other synthetic drugs.

2009: The U.S. government stops using the term the "War on Drugs." The government will channel some of the billions of dollars spent on the drug war each year and use the money for drug prevention and treatment programs, which have shown success in reducing drug use.

A sign in Florida shows that anyone caught using, selling, or possessing drugs in a local park will be severely punished.

Rules about taking drugs must have come about for the same reasons we have drug laws today. Individuals who became drug dependent could not be healthy, productive members of their societies.

became a social problem. Factories needed alert workers who would arrive on time six days a week. Government and religious groups blamed much of the urban crime and poverty of this period on alcohol. There was a growing movement to limit alcohol use or ban it altogether.

From the late 1870s to around 1920, British and American social leaders tried to shut down saloons and ban alcohol. Male drunkenness was an increasing threat to family life. In 1920,

Female members of the Anti-Saloon League smash up a saloon in 1897.

the United States passed the Eighteenth Amendment, outlawing the manufacture of alcohol. The amendment was repealed in 1933. Prohibition laws could not be enforced because so many people were making and selling alcohol illegally.

Preventive efforts started to shift beyond laws. Alcoholics Anonymous (AA), an antidrinking organization, was founded in 1935. To this day, AA helps alcohol-dependent people regain their independence from this drug.

OPIOID DEPENDENCE

Evidence from ancient human bones, seeds, and tools indicates that early humans discovered the opium sap of wild poppy flowers around 4000 B.C.E. Opium cultivation made its way from the Middle East to India and then to China and Japan.

It appears that for thousands of years, opium was restricted to use in religious ceremonies or for medical purposes. Opium made it possible for doctors to perform surgery and to ease patients' pain. These restrictions did not keep opium from the general population, however, and people began to become opium dependent.

By the mid–1700s, opium dependence and addiction were widespread in Asia. By the 1800s, the drug trade in opium was practically unstoppable in most parts of the world. Both medical and illicit uses of morphine and heroin continued into the twentieth century and to this day.

By the early part of the twentieth century, heroin addiction had become a huge public health problem in the United States. In 1909, the U.S. government outlawed the import of raw opium. In 1914, Congress passed the Harrison Narcotics Act, which made it a crime for anyone to use or sell opium-based drugs except for medical purposes.

The abuse of prescription opioids, as well as other prescription drugs, became another public health problem in the 1950s and 1960s. Drug companies introduced new opioid products quickly, often without fully testing the possibility for causing drug dependence. To deal with opioid drug dependence and addiction, the federal government passed the Controlled Substance Act in 1970. According to this law, drugs are rated and controlled in terms of their safety, usefulness, and potential for dependence and addiction.

COCAINE DEPENDENCE

In the 1500s and 1600s, when Spanish explorers arrived in what is now South America, they observed that natives chewed on the leaves of the coca plants that grew in the mountains. In leaf form, coca probably served as a mild stimulant. It curbed appetites in an area where food was scarce.

In 1860, a scientist named Albert Neiman isolated cocaine. This concentrated form of the coca plant had immediate medical use as an anesthetic. Countries around the world began to grow coca plants for medical use. Some doctors used cocaine to help addicts conquer morphine addiction. Later, manufacturers added cocaine to tobacco and to the original version of Coca-Cola. These practices stopped in 1903, as health providers began to realize the dangers of cocaine dependence and addiction.

In 1914, the passage of the Harrison Narcotic Act in the United States put cocaine under regulation. This has not stopped cocaine dependence, however. Officials in the United States estimate that 2 million Americans are addicted to cocaine. It is a major cause of drug-related emergency room visits.

NICOTINE DEPENDENCE

Nicotine has a less ancient history than alcohol, opium, and cocaine. In what is now South America, native people probably domesticated two types of tobacco plants thousands of years ago. When Christopher Columbus landed in the New World in 1492, he found native people smoking wherever they went. In his 1492 journal, Columbus reported, "These two Christians met many [native] people on the road . . . the men always with a firebrand [cigarette] in their hands, and certain herbs to take their smokes."

Nicotine dependence started right away among the early Spanish missionaries who traveled to the New World after

Columbus. Authorities passed laws forbidding tobacco smoking during church services. Because nicotine was so addictive, people could make a lot of money by exporting it. Nicotine made its way from the New World to the rest of the world faster than any drug substance ever has. Dependence spread quickly as well. Governments tried to control tobacco for more than four hundred years without much success.

Smoking is banned in many public places today, including restaurants and bars.

Health problems soon followed nicotine dependence and addiction. By the 1920s, doctors in the United States began to report high rates of heart disease and cancers of all kinds among smokers. In the 1950s, the U.S. surgeon general and the American Cancer Society acknowledged that smoking was a major health problem. A 1964 presidential report stated that cigarette smoking was the major cause of lung cancer, several other types of cancer, heart disease, and breathing problems. Prior to the report, nearly 50 percent of Americans smoked. After the report, that number decreased to about 30 percent for the next thirty years or so.

After 1964, many other antismoking measures helped further reduce the percentage of smokers in the United States. Today, about 20 to 25 percent of the American population smokes. Antismoking measures have included public health advertisements, high cigarette taxes, warning labels, age restrictions, and strict limits on public smoking. All have made it difficult for smokers to afford their habit and to enjoy it socially.

4

FROM DRUG DEPENDENCE TO INDEPENDENCE

Here is some good news: most young people never become drug dependent. They never take drugs at all, or perhaps try drugs and stop. Most young people who drink alcohol do so in moderation when they are old enough to drink legally. According to the National Institute on Drug Abuse (NIDA), rates of illicit use of nearly all drugs dropped during the last two decades. Fewer students in grades eight, ten, and twelve smoke cigarettes or marijuana or drink alcohol than students in those grades did twenty years ago. Today's eighth graders get the biggest applause for not taking up smoking the way eighth graders did in previous years. Since nicotine is a gateway drug, fewer new smokers will probably lead to less dependence on other drugs later.

So why did most drug use rates go down? Many of today's preteens and teens get the message that early drug use has many negative effects. Also, many teens who successfully resist taking drugs get through the most tempting years by taking advice from parents, older siblings and friends, teachers, family doctors, and youth leaders. A caring older person is more likely than a fellow teen to say, "Hey, maybe taking strange pills prescribed for somebody else is not such a great idea" or "Sniffing vapors out of an aerosol can that kills bugs probably kills a few brain cells, too."

But there is some bad news. Rates of inhalant use have not dropped as much as rates for most other drugs. Among drug-taking teens, prescription drug abuse remains a problem. Opioids such as OxyContin and Vicodin are way too easy to find without a prescription. It is also fairly easy to access tranquilizers such as Xanax and Valium or sedatives such as Ritalin and Adderall. Still, most preteens and teens have figured out that their own natural brain chemistry and some healthy sleep, exercise, and eating habits will keep them relaxed or focused. Professional help is available for teens who struggle with depression, other mood disorders, or ADHD.

WHO IS AT RISK FOR DRUG DEPENDENCE?

Experts say that drug users at risk for dependence share certain characteristics long before they take their first drink,

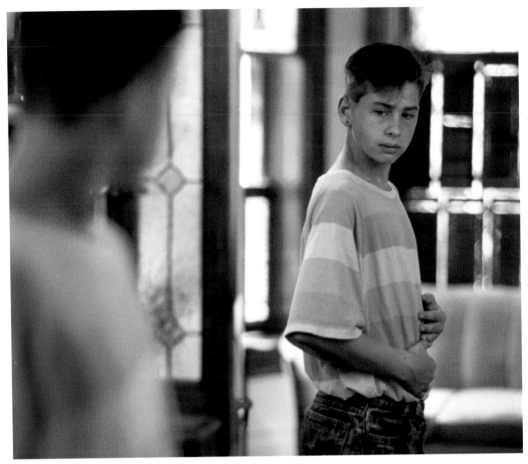

People may abuse drugs for many reasons, including low self-esteem.

cigarette, or marijuana joint. Studies of children and preteens have shown that future drug users may have some of the following tendencies:

- They seek new sensations.
- They have trouble controlling excitability and anger.
- They feel depressed.
- They have a poor self-image.

- They take big risks at an early age.
- They have social problems within the family and at school.
- They have trouble postponing rewards.
- They come from overly unstructured or overly strict homes.
- They have a sibling or a parent who abuses drugs.
- They have been verbally, physically, or sexually abused.
- Their parents do not send caring and frequent antidrug messages.

The brains of drug users may turn out to be different from the brains of people who do not become drug dependent. Studies show that some depressed people have fewer receptors for the brain's natural "feel-good" neurotransmitters—opioid, serotonin, and dopamine. Someone with fewer receptors may be especially vulnerable to drugs that flood the brain with these neurotransmitters.

Does that mean depressed or moody people are doomed to become drug dependent? The answer is no. Help is available for preteens and teens who suffer from depression, other mood disorders, or ADHD. Community clinics, schools, doctors, and psychologists can help young people cope with emotional difficulties without using cigarettes, alcohol, marijuana, and other drugs.

Excuses, Excuses

. . . .

The first time a young teen is offered a drug—and usually that drug is alcohol—can be a shock. It can happen as soon as fourth grade or early middle school. That is when parties start happening or preteens start hanging out at one another's houses when adults are not home or are not paying attention.

Although most illicit drug use is going down, today's adolescents are likely to know other teens who use drugs. But drug takers are in the minority. In 2008, about 60 percent of eighth graders did *not* try alcohol in the previous year. Seventy-nine percent of eighth graders did *not* try cigarettes. And about 90 percent of eight graders *never* tried marijuana.

To stay on the sober side, what should you say and do to avoid drugs at any age? Ask yourself, "Is it safe? Is it smart? Is it legal?" If it is not safe, smart, or legal, then the best two-word answer to a beer, a joint, or a bunch of pills is simple: "No thanks." You never owe somebody an explanation of why you do not want to put chemicals inside your body.

DO I HAVE A PROBLEM?

How do drug users know when they have become dependent? Here are some questions drug users should ask themselves:

- Is the drug I am taking illegal for my age?
- Do I need more of the drug than I used to?
- Do most of my friends use drugs?
- Do I use the drug more often or for a longer time than I planned to?
- Do I keep trying to cut back or quit but fail?
- Do I spend a lot of time thinking about when I can take the drug again?
- Do I spend a lot of time trying to get the drug, getting money to buy it, using it, or recovering from using it?
- Has anyone told me that my drug use is a problem?

Taking illegal drugs for the first time can seem less forbidden when a close friend starts using drugs.

- Does my drug use interfere with school or responsibilities at home?
- Does my drug use make my problems worse?

If you answered yes to any of these questions, you may be drug dependent. It is time to get some help. When you are dependent on a drug, quitting is not easy. However, staying drug dependent is much harder.

QUITTING TIME

Researchers of substance abuse have learned a lot about the best methods for ending drug dependence.

Many people think that going into rehabilitation, or "rehab," is the only successful way to get off drugs. However, rehabilitation programs are designed for drug addicts. Drug-dependent users can try simpler steps first in order to slow down their dependence before they quit for good. Many of the steps involve making adjustments at home, in school, and with friends to create a supportive environment for quitting. Here are some ways to get on the path to drug independence:

- Cut back on the amount of time you spend with friends who use drugs. Increase the amount of time you spend with friends who do not use drugs.
- Take up some kind of physical activity before actually setting a date to quit using drugs.

One way of trying to stop using drugs is by meditating and clearing the mind.

Teens in Florida attend a picnic sponsored by a Drug Free Youth program.

- Learn a new skill that channels or eases anxiety—dancing, knitting, playing an instrument, cooking, painting, writing poetry, or composing music.
- Learn relaxation techniques, such as visualization of calming scenes, deep breathing, meditation, and stretching.
- Develop better sleep habits by getting to bed earlier and at the same time every night. Lack of sleep seriously affects depression and moods.

- Think about taking a babysitting, lifeguard training, or camp-counseling course to experience positive feelings of responsibility.
- Volunteer at an organization such as a hospital, nursing home, environmental group, or soup kitchen.
- Spend time with adults you trust. Ask them what they think about drugs.
- Start hanging out a little more often with favorite brothers, sisters, parents, or other relatives to get that supportive family feeling.
- If you are a risk taker, as many drug users are, see if there is a stimulating activity you can do within a well-supervised group. Rock climbing, mountain biking, backcountry skiing or camping, wind or ocean surfing, and skiing are all activities known to rev up adventurous young people.
- Once a few positive changes are in place, set a date for quitting the drug. Before that date, cut back so there is less of the drug to quit. Ask a trusted friend to help you reach your goal.
- Set simple, small "baby step" goals instead of huge goals that are hard to meet. Your goal might be not having a cigarette for a single day. Or it might be going to the gym on Friday afternoons instead of to a classmate's house where people drink alcohol. Then add another baby

step. If you slip back, try again the same day.

- Attend a teen drug-dependence support group. Some of the most successful drug-prevention groups are run for teens by teens. One of the best is Students Against Destructive Decisions (SADD), as well as Alcoholics Anonymous and Narcotics Anonymous (NA) groups for teens.
- Ask your family doctor or school counselor about how to get help. You can speak to them confidentially.

Independence from drugs is like any kind of independence. It is a great feeling that lasts and lasts.

GLOSSARY

addict—A drug user who is both physically and psychologically dependent on a drug.

alcohol—A liquid that has depressive effects on the brain and body.

amphetamine—A manufactured stimulant that increases alertness and heightens mood.

anxiety—An overwhelming feeling of worry and nervousness, often without a realistic cause.

attention-deficit/hyperactivity disorder (ADHD)—A condition that makes it difficult for someone to concentrate and to feel calm.

binge drinking—Drinking four or five alcoholic drinks within an hour or so.

blood-brain barrier—A thin, protective covering that keeps many harmful substances from getting into the brain.

caffeine—A chemical stimulant in most types of coffee, tea, chocolate, energy drinks, and many soft drinks.

central nervous system (CNS)—The system of nerves in the brain and spinal cord.

cocaine—A highly addictive stimulant made from the coca plant.

dependent—The craving of a chemical substance or habit despite the harm it may cause.

depressant—A drug that slows down the body's activities,

such as breathing, blood flow, heartbeat, muscle movement,
speech, and judgment.

depression—Ongoing feelings of deep unhappiness.

dopamine—A brain chemical that carries messages to other
cells and triggers pleasurable feelings.

drug—A chemical substance, often illegal, that causes changes
in the brain.

euphoria—A feeling of excitement and great happiness.

ferment—To use a chemical process to change plant sugars
into alcohol.

frontal lobe—A late-developing part of the brain involved in
judgment, planning, and decision making.

gamma-aminobutyric acid (GABA)—A natural chemical in
the brain that slows down the brain's activities.

gateway drug—A drug, such as nicotine, that may lead to
the use of other drugs.

hallucinations—Imaginary perceptions of something that does
not exist in reality.

hallucinogen—A substance that changes how the senses
interpret sounds, sights, odors, textures, and tastes.

heroin—A highly addictive, pain-relieving drug made from
poppies.

homeostasis—A chemically balanced state in a healthy
organism.

hormones—Natural or manufactured chemical substances
involved in regulating the body's activities.

illicit—Illegal or medically unapproved.

inhalants—The vapors of certain chemical substances.

marijuana—A chemical substance made from the *Cannabis sativa* plant, which produces relaxation, mood change, and a heightening of the senses.

methamphetamine—A highly addictive stimulant that produces intense reactions in the user's mood and senses.

morphine—A calming but highly addictive painkiller made from opium.

narcotics—Usually opium-based drugs that relieve pain by dulling the senses and producing a deep feeling of calm.

neurons—Nerve cells found in the brain and spinal cord.

neurotransmitters—Nerve cell chemicals that send messages to activate other cells.

nicotine—The harmful ingredient in tobacco that creates dependency and addiction.

nucleus accumbens—A part of the brain that responds to rewards.

opioids—Drugs made from the poppy plant or from manufactured copies of opium.

opium—A substance made from part of a poppy flower and used to make morphine, heroin, or manufactured opioids.

panic attacks—Sudden episodes of great anxiety, breathlessness, and unreality.

pleasure circuit—A cell network in the lower part of the brain through which dopamine travels to produce pleasurable sensations.

prescription—A doctor's written medical order for a drug.

psychoactive—Influencing feelings and thoughts.

psychological—Relating to the mind.

receptors—The points on a cell where drug chemicals or neurotransmitters attach.

sedatives—Chemical substances that slow down activities, such as breathing, heartbeat, and movement, and that may bring on sleep.

seizures—Bursts of abnormal brain activity that set off sudden bodily changes, such as twitching, uncontrolled muscle contractions, or bizarre feelings and thoughts.

serotonin—A neurotransmitter involved in moods.

steroids—Natural or manufactured substances that affect growth and sexual development.

stimulants—Drugs that temporarily speed up activities, such as breathing, heartbeat, blood flow, and thoughts.

tolerance—The body's adjustment to a drug's effects, resulting in the need for increased doses to produce the drug's original strong effect.

tranquilizers—Drugs that bring about a state of calm and lack of resistance.

withdrawal—The end of drug use, which may trigger unpleasant reactions as the body tries to cope with the absence of a drug.

FIND OUT MORE

Books

Karr, Justin. *Drug Abuse.* Social Issues Firsthand series. Farmington Hills, MI: Greenhaven Press, 2007.

Klosterman, Lorrie. *Drugs and the Body.* Tarrytown, NY: Marshall Cavendish, 2007.

Koellhoffer, Tara, and Ronald Brogan, Introduction. *Inhalants and Solvents.* Junior Drug Awareness series. New York: Chelsea House, 2008.

Kuhn, Cynthia, et al. *Buzzed: The Straight Facts about the Most Used and Abused Drugs from Alcohol to Ecstasy*, 3rd ed. New York: W. W. Norton & Company, 2008.

Organizations and Websites

Alcoholics Anonymous is a twelve-step program for people who are dependent on alcohol:
www.aa.org

Families Anonymous is a twelve-step program for families with a drug- or alcohol-dependent member:
www.familiesanonymous.org

neurons, 13, **14**, 16, 23
neurotransmitters, 13, 23, 25–26, 47
nicotine dependence, 6-9, 41–43, 44
    effects of, 17, 19–22, **20**, 31

opioid dependence, 28–29, 45, 47
    history of, 34, **36**, 39–40, 41
overdosing, 29

painkiller dependence, 28–29
pleasure circuit (brain), 13–15, 19, 23,
    31, 47
pot. *See* marijuana dependence
prescription drugs' dependence, **22**,
    22–23, 45
prohibition laws (U.S.), 39

sedative dependence, 28–29, 45
serotonin, 13, 47
smoking. *See* cigarette smoking;
    marijuana dependence
speed. *See* amphetamine dependence
steroid dependence, 9–11, **11**, 33
stimulant dependence, 17–19, **18**, 20, 23

tobacco, 20, 34, 41, 42
tolerance, 16, 29
tranquilizer dependence, 28–29, 45

weed. *See* marijuana dependence

withdrawal symptoms, 8, 11, 12

ABOUT THE AUTHOR

L. H. Colligan writes about many topics, from study skills to activity books and children's fiction. She once worked for a health foundation that promoted exercise, healthy eating, and regular sleeping habits as the best ways to live drug free. She enjoys hiking, biking, and yoga. She lives in Western Massachusetts.